Heres a

Poems from a life

From 'Here and Now:'

Enjoy, oh do enjoy
The hereness and the nowness of it.
Whatever is beyond, behind
Be, if you must, aware of
But not too much – no more than serves
To measure by, to savour by
To live by grace within
The here and now.

It is the clumsy man we too much are
That cannot delicately hold the time
Within his juggling mind
And commandeer the chasing heart
Softly to send the blood like fingers
To touch and know the living hour
And store it richly by.

each waking one of us is poet

David Henschel in 1985

Heres and Nows

Poems from a life

David Henschel

*edited with a foreword by Martin Dace, with
additional material by
Norah Henschel and John Torrance*

Narrow Gate Press
London MMX

Dedicated by the editor to David and Norah Henschel, inspired teachers and wonderful friends.

Published by Narrow Gate Press,
24 Frederick Square, London SE16 5XR, England

www.narrow-gate.co.uk

Cover image: David Henschel
Cover design: Martin Dace

ISBN: 978-0-9565497-0-9

Foreword

I have made this book of David's poems so that they will not be lost.

They are verses of a kind that can encourage thoughts more useful than our habitual ones, and bring depth to ordinary events. Our real lives are full of depth, but we seldom see it.

If a poem is emotion recollected in tranquillity, then the poet must have been present to the emotion, to the moment, to *the hereness and the nowness of it* as David says. This is why we need artists and poets, to bring us back to ourselves, *here*. A good poem cannot come solely from imagination, but from reality itself, well-experienced and therefore well-remembered.

Our lives are made up mostly of ordinary things:

> *Sun in the morning kitchen*
> *Rings the day's bell clear and lively*
> *Sings with the frying sizzle*
> *The tap's swish*
> *The kettle's hiss and bubble.*

.

...and the poet, like a still-life painter, may bring us to what was already there:

> *This workshed is the place…*
> *I'll lend my spirit's eyes till yours begin to be awake.*

and show us what we are sometimes too fast to see:

I swear that hyacinth dances, and I'm not alas drunk.

> *I've been sitting and watching that bowl's green*
> *lances*
> *Curving and swaying, the curled white heads*
> *prancing*
> *Like foam in the breeze from the top of a wave.*

> *You will say they are still.*
> *Does that stop them from moving?*

Sometimes the places seen and felt are not so common. The storeroom in the museum at Besançon brings us:

> *…Ammonites and Attic vases busts statues*
> *Flinthead arrowtips sarcophagi*
> *And one small quiet Egyptian*
> *Three thousand years in mouldering swathes*
> *Lies chill as the winter.*

– or Le Corbusier's church of Notre Dame, modern architecture, its uncompromising concrete and glass bringing a powerful and unexpected message. (To extract from that poem is to break it, but you will find it in this book.)

If we are awake to our moments, common and uncommon, then:

> *...each waking one of us is poet*
> *and may utter hope*
> *as confidently as the Pope.*

Then there are the reflective, philosophical poems:

> *You are adrift. – I tell you*
> *You are adrift and do not know it.*

> *– Towards what bourne then are you going*
> *In this no longer rimmed confusion?*
> *Do you have lodestone, compass, map*
> *Recognise stars to steer by?*
> *What do you do when winds*
> *Pull every which way whirling thoughts –*
> *Let down your anchors? What anchors*
> *Have you, engines, oars in case of breakdown*
> *Lifeboats do you carry? Indeed*
> *What flag or flags do you sail under –*
> *Only old bones' anarchy and ending?*

Do not expect David to give the answer. But he leaves us enough space to live the question.

A poet must use words, yet for all their beauty there is a trap in words, even in our best eloquence. We live in wordy imagination, as though the words, mere tokens, were the things themselves. Words pin things down, limit them, and the reality slips away behind the game of language.

> *When the eye listens*
> *The tongue is blinded...*

> *...Yet I perceive all speech*
> *Like all translation*
> *Is defeat...*

and:

> *In the language of eyes only*
> *Have I truly spoken to you.*

Even so, words are the poet's tools. Like the ideas which they express, the poet's words, and indeed our own words if we try, can point beyond themselves, so that the poet's skill, our skill, can make a wordless music out of them.

The poet, like any craftsman, must be a master his or her craft. There is discipline in these lines: not that it shouts at you, but it is there, supporting the ear sometimes with unobtrusive rhythm and rhyme, sometimes with inner echoes and alliteration. There is structure. Read a poem out loud and you will hear it.

And you – whoever recognise
a kind of beauty, any place
in anything where eye or ear discerned
and touched with them in turn
your spirit with the laughing wand
have also waked, and passed beyond.

What is the laughing wand? Who touches our spirit with it? And if the poet does, then through whose agency? And if our eyes and ears open to us for a moment the brighter world of our own waking spirit, then each of us will become a restless searcher until we either forget or arrive.

Finally, there is the poet's desire to pass on both the finding and the searching:

This is no land of milk and honey quiet.
Only the restless searchers come
here drawing words like water from
deep wells below their spirits' hills:
a joy too much like pain
yearning to be given
in others
birth again.

Enjoy.

- Martin Dace, London 2010

❧

Acknowledgements

The editor is indebted to Norah Henschel for her kind permission to allow me to edit David's poems for publication, for permission to reproduce two of her own poems in this volume, and for her advice and encouragement throughout the project.

I am also indebted to John Torrance for permission to reproduce his poem *Dimensions of remembrance*.

Thanks are also due to both Norah Henschel and John Torrance for proof-reading. Any remaining errors and omissions are solely the responsibility of the editor.

David Henschel's poems are ordered exactly as I found them in his bound typescript.

14

Contents

The last lesson

In what's remaining
Lies the last wilderness of time.

Hours run through my ribs like sand
And turn to snow.
I, having traced my circle, stand
And in their fertile fusion sow
Roses of solitude.

Those who approach the promised land
Must know
Some way to make sand
Grow
Learn
How to make snow
Burn.

A piece of the maine?

Go to another man and show him –
"This I've just written, tell me what you think."
He'll say "Oh yes, how nice" and take the scrip
To use the eyes and hide the doubtful lip.

Why should he otherwise?
Whose many headed self preoccupies
His secret entrances,
Whose thoughts' continual tide
I have attempted to divide
And march my feelings like an exiled band
Into communion's promised land.

For summer work early

For summer work early
In the iron lattice of a railway bridge
A dove warbling, silly with morning,
Fulfilled the golden promise of the day
With a chuckle of audible sunbeams,
Before, on my dawdling-beneath road,
The slumbering seal
Shook off the long grey shade
Of shuttered houses, snuffed the blue air
And on its warming back, wheels
Of my bicycle spinning from my toes,
Rode me like one who in his private fair
Juggled a ball of sunlight on his nose.

Dylan Thomas: on re-reading Fern Hill

I'd normally speak more plain but
fountains and fanfares and
fireworks are lovely to word with
and who can escape that infection when
reading him: fireworks of fireworking
words let them
be his.

Who would have thought –
though recollect the Socratic loaf
also divinely leavened –
behind that dumpy face that fizz and frenzy,
behind that cottage lump the rising yeast,
within the beery oaf that
shattering pulse of sight
those suns in splendour, sounds
of sudden song, euphoniums
from elephantine Africas
and bells like angels swinging
in laughing gales across the ringing hills

and always the springing of wordy winey water
profound from wells of running light – which
suddenly somehow sank beneath the
everlasting night
leaving again God wondered at
such eucharists to feast us with
and as we belch to filch.

Street passing

Why did you look at me like that
Dark girl I passed in the wet street?
Was it the faintest of mockery
Returning my glance, or barely perceptible
Wrinkle of friendliness I saw
Never now discoverable?

I stepped from the narrow pavement's
Chisel dimpled kerb to the seal back road;
We passed, between the gray walls' austere
    stone
The glistening surface grew wide behind us:
Neither looked back.

You warmed, and chilled, and pass me in my
    mind
Again a dark girl in a wet street;
And I remembering you with tightened eyes
To bring back every detail of the scene
Am wrung with anguish at the lack of even
Finger tip to tip or word's one contact.

I know in time to come a long way off
The sense of loss will come again like rain.

Three sketches sitting by the river
(King's 'Backs', Cambridge)

1. All strangers who smile

I know nothing more
Surely of the present
Than a stranger's
Unexpected smile.

The past stays in
Future attends
Corner and antechamber
Of the mind

But the smile
From nowhere out of nothing
Flies like that sparrow from dark to dark
Through Northumbria's royal hall
Converting the present heart
For more than its fire-lit while –

Thank you all
Strangers who smile.

*(The reference is to St. Paulinus's conversion of King
Edwin of Northumbria, 625 A.D. – see Bede's His-
tory of England.)*

24

2. Prospero bettered

Father and son walked by
holding hands
the elder balding, face lined, yet
showing in the boy's clear face
spring hair and summer-coming feet
as once he was.

At first I smiled at this; then
saddened by time's evidence my
'third thought was my grave.'

But who would languish there –
the fourth was like the first and surer
for the sense of what lives on
despite the single death: perhaps
to better Prospero every fourth thought
should be brave.

Confirming worth
came sun with shadow patterning
the present path.

3. *She came by fast*

She came by fast, all legs and hair
almost no skirt at all
and sat down quickly on the grass
her back against the sunny wall.

She'd made quite surely for that spot.

Now
she overlooks
the high green avenue
the low green lawn
the ruffled pewter stream
the arching bridge, willows and beech
and boats and swimming ducks and two
black strolling nuns only the wind
wild in their habit
and children running by
one placid bird upon the grass
pecking its feathers
refusing to panic.

A punt slides past, the fellow
taking snapshots – of the buildings
not the girl
though she is pretty

with legs like swans' necks
and hair of blown straw.

Now where, I wonder,
did she come from so fast
to sit by herself so determinedly?

Truth is the daughter of Time

When I was young
I thought it fine
To write like wine.
Now I am older, know Time's daughter
And try to write like water.

When I was young
My fiery mind would say
Display
Your talents and your graces.
But now my spirit tells my face
Look with grace
As though life is
A cheerful place.

So blithe an exhortation?
Or so stern.
So soon
Sanded with anger, or with sorrow;
Yet who does not know
A truth so simple should prevail

Though on the desert man the rains will fail
He knows where life springs, he will not forget

And if he seek, and love, that daughter
He may strike rock
And summon water.

Corbusier: Notre Dame du Haut

Has said only and exactly
What he wanted
Poem in concrete and glass.
May my words so.

Tricorne, concave, pyramidal
Shape to hold
Like a hand
And launch
Space
Breathtaking falcon;
To catch and cut and colour
Light
Shape shadow.

Solid in flight
Yet rooted and horizoned
Man's, yet
God belonging:
Embracing, accepting, dismissing
A single universal gesture
Arm, palm, wings
One benison
High hill to hills, pilgrims, skies
And sun saluting.
One message

Choose

Here and Now

Enjoy, oh do enjoy
The hereness and the nowness of it.
Whatever is beyond, behind
Be, if you must, aware of
But not too much – no more than serves
To measure by, to savour by
To live by grace within
The here and now.

It is the clumsy man we too much are
That cannot delicately hold the time
Within his juggling mind
And commandeer the chasing heart
Softly to send the blood like fingers
To touch and know the living hour
And store it richly by.

One day we die.
They say we scan
In the last living moments all our span.
We'd wish, I think, to go to Death
Or God
Like guests with gifts
Remembered and collected from our store
Of heres and nows
And say:

This trust of life's fulfilled,
This gift's returned, with more I found:
I was not poor.

**Storeroom: Musée des Beaux Arts
Besançon**

Shacked up lofty dusty racks
Store paintings by
– Anyhow hung –
Courbet Goya Fragonard
Rembrandt Rubens Titian la Tour ...

Only the little written dockets
Assist the astonished guess
To tell these treasures from
What seemed neglected daubs.

Close by them
Ammonites and Attic vases busts statues
Flinthead arrowtips sarcophagi
And one small quiet Egyptian
Three thousand years in mouldering swathes
Lies chill as the winter.

I can almost touch him with one hand
A Rembrandt with the other.

And in the dark racks further back
Joseph bends still to drill his wood
By candleflame that la Tour loved

His cupped hand luminous with light
The young Christ holds above the undone work
    ...

And the little dead Egyptian
Sleeping beneath the glowing paint
Quite unaware of that awakening.

New castles in the air

With what delight when small
And often into less illusioned youth
I made my senses take upon the air
The stolid limbs that only bounced the bed
And soared with leaping heart among the
        houses
Flew bending races round the chimney pots
Or through the winter branches.

And all my movements were of air
With dances made of curves like clouds
Of gusts of jumps like sudden leaves
Of swallow swoops, a gull's sea-low parabola
Of lines like leaning grasses on the heath
Or wide savannahs in a picture book.

Something of Peter Pan in every man - but then
I was so little used, I think, to flesh
It seemed quite learnable to trust the air.
It may have been. I did not study how to keep
The gracious possibilities of youth;
And now I know I cannot fly,
That all my thoughts are slouched with earth
Where they were touched with air.

And yet – I cannot leave the matter there.
The child who surges still within the man
Has urged his upward bending to the stars
Of knowledge that has taken him from youth.
Some watcher sitting guard upon the dials,
Co-mates asleep, the humming exile
Flaring, surprised, the everlasting night,
May catch another sight of innocence
Before they build new castles in the air
Beyond no more the dreamers' moon.

The baby

I lie like a shell receiving murmurs
Still now on a new shore.

Noises and language a lilt of strange cadences
Flow in the household tides of business
And ebb into stranger stillnesses ...

Some vaguest memory of this
Seashore lapping of existence
Will one day blur the edges of a thought
Or touch my dreams with symbols
Of unfathomable mystery
Out of this first land venture of creation

And I full geared and striding
Whither now unknown
Will murmur recognition
My mind turned inward on my buried seas.

Res poetica

A poem is organic
waits
until it has to be
or die.

Conceived of a thing and a thought
the idea stirs in the mind's womb
assembling words like limbs
or hymns to praise with.

Let it lie.
Minutes or days
or the subterranean year may
bring it the amaze of birth.

But truths imagined in our human earth
have roots uneven, bear
uncertain fruits, or disappear
unwordfleshed into air.

Each waking one of us

I had been thinking like a falling leaf ...
Windshocked, the turning tired days
shuffled me sere and cynical
into my gutter.

I wish I could remember what or who
– a debt is due –
recalled rejoicably when read what roused
my first green sap and sent me
shooting into spring.
I only know I rediscovered how
each waking one of us is poet
and may utter hope
as confidently as the Pope.

And I remembered early time:
how growing green with dancing days
and first love like a kicking child
I had a sudden simple vision
saw creation whole and one
outrippling from the first star
dropped like a pebble in the pool of space
– and how I laughed, no choice,
as when I heard my father tell
in youth he heard a mathematics master greet
Pythagoras' perfection of a truth

for pupils with delight and wonderment:
his subject was his garden
its poetry his voice.

But now I do not see so simple clear;
something is lost which was fresh air
which washed where now I long to reach
behind the eyes and gave the mind
a winded hawk's horizon.
Now it seeks to cut its leash of doubt
and fear with lesser but still certainties
which more besides can seize – to find
and warm ourselves in common kind.

And you – whoever recognise
a kind of beauty, any place
in anything where eye or ear discerned
and touched with them in turn
your spirit with the laughing wand
have also waked, and passed beyond.

As for myself, this being said,
a debt, although I can't be sure who earned
it, may be being paid.

Ars phoenix

So – when the spirit moves, create:
Breed lovelier with chisels or with paint
Beyond the form mix beauties undelineate:
With art inseminate the things that
Outfly nature's known restraint.

Do what you will with words: reflame
In blessed language what your life has said
Which meant beyond the moment when it came
Within time's frame, that words within your
    race
May run like blood long after you are bled.

Is this one?

Sometime I haven't
you haven't
a poem
I mean, written,

Wonder is this one?
You may.
It is.
Why? Because no other
could be
the yearning to become
as undefined yet certain as
the earlystirring womb.

Greet me any reader
for I am your
like mine before
unborn or even
waiting still to be
        conceived.
Find me where I may yet be
within.

[Begin...

Begin.
It may
have no proper
scheme of rhyme
nor regularly scan.
But if it is
you can.

This rose

This rose, this red rose –
See how each petal
On petal is certainly folded
Turned to the mould of a small minaret:
The hard-wound pointed heart of the rose
Piercing delight with wonder.

Just this notice now:
See how each petal curls at the collar
Glowing with carefully graded colour,
Black bloomed purple to blood bloomed
    crimson
Perfectly matched
The work of a craftsman.

Bowl of white hyacinths

I swear that hyacinth dances, and I'm not alas
    drunk.

I've been sitting and watching that bowl's green
    lances
Curving and swaying, the curled white heads
    prancing
Like foam in the breeze from the top of a wave.

You will say – they are still.
Does that stop them from moving?
Don't you know how

The wind in the corn in a painting can ripple
And shadow with sunlight swing under the
    trees
Or a ballet girl frou-frou'd remain in a brush
    stroke
Perpetually mobile?
I say they are dancing, their stillness illusion

– That, drunken or sober, remains my conclu-
    sion.

Sun in the morning kitchen

Sun in the morning kitchen
Rings the day's bell clear and lively
Sings with the frying sizzle
The tap's swish
The kettle's hiss and bubble.

Sun on the bathroom sill
Laps into the water
Dappling the white basin
Mingles with the tingling chill's
Slap on the sleepy skin
Soaks the eyelids blood redgold
Down to the heart's roots
Fresher than mountain springs.
Between cold gasps I whistle
The ever singing Mozart.

Sun at the house stones
And tracing grass shadows on the path;
After breakfast
Back to the warming wall
Eyes shut.
I sit in gold and orange
Listening to the wind.

You young man

Which of your many will you choose
To follow like a path into the
Everlasting?
You young man, what
Self enthrone and crown with cares to come
And orb with joys undawned upon?
Where will you have your feet, how
Dance like Brandenburgs, with
What dishes of the soul seek to be replete?

Too soon, you say, to think of which
Or know how many.

Too rich
You are that one day come
To spending's end;
Whose path, from dandelion fields
Down dunes across the windy strand
Becomes sea drowned
And footprints whether danced or
Stumbled tides make level in the sand.

Suntan

I lay wind cold waiting.
Clouds passed, sky came
The sun that on my face at first
Hit like a fist
Grew soon a lover's seeking mouth
About my eyes and cheeks and lips
Burning my ears like passion thoughts.

All kisses through the flesh
Blood bathed and ran about my body
Inspiring roots that sunflower upwards shot
Like words that seek their poetry
Or spirit uncorruption's grace.

Now
Brown as the ozone poster months before
Upon a sootgrime station wall
Which beckoned wishfully to southern suns
I quit my cell of winter self
And lent this grace which makes the mirror kind
Obscuring records of time's other stains
Awhile ignore the witness who remains
The inner witness of the mind.

A very private love affair

I put your letter in a file
marked Personal
and shut the cabinet.
It felt so weird
I hover between amusement
and an aching sorrow.
How symbolic of the reasonable act's
irrelevance and incongruity
against which the heart cries out
its pain in laughter.

See
(but you cannot...)
how vividly your words flow in my blood
lighten my eyes and lift my mouth:
what a ridiculous act
to put them in a filing cabinet
– even though the file is marked
marked
(how indelibly marked)
Personal.

Old age

How often old age
Achieves the beauty of accomplishment.
In lines of clear enigma
Time's translation writes down what was said
By tongues of passion, or of pain, or peace
In languages of longing, loving, learning,
Learning forgetting,
Forgetting
What was once done.

That it is done
Is so simple an idea to live with
It gives the face – time's page, like paper –
Transparency
And one may look through the eyes
Into stillness.

After the working day

After the working day, time
Tightens the eyes, ticking off
Tasks to be or half done till
It presses them shut as sundown.

Where once when younger
Each moment like buds to the light
Was always an opening newly on wonders,
Seek now fresh vision of the known –

Let it be peaceful to you; let it say
'Here is the quietness you have sought today'
– The thing your eye, your body easing in the
    chair
Its day recoiling through the veins like sleep,
First glances on with pleasure and rests there ...

Touch your spirit coolly with the things you
    keep.

Moth

There fell, here flutters
White moth,
Night late, lamp lit
Bedside.
New moon was but is not
Now where only blackness shutters
Owls utter and a low
Wind flusters the curtains
Through which the moths
Come stuttering.

This flew
White
Flattering the stiff electric stare
With its own frail embattled light –

Of which it lacked the outward sense
And inner sight
Rather to dare its wings against
What must have seemed
But could not prove
The endless night.

A fine Whitsunday

In thy church, this garden, Lord
Receive my thanks and bless my thoughts.
Do not curse these flowers with
The binding weeds of shoulds and oughts.

The sunshine and the shadow pace
Processional across the lawn
Like years and seasons in their course
Smiling and frowning in my face.

My children come to sit with me;
Read and chatter, pick a flower.
Like anglers by a quiet stream
We fish for peace, and catch the hour.

The sap runs sweetly, a green blood
In which we hold communion now
Hearing the teaching of the wind
And long responses of the bough

Whose fingers break the golden bread
Scattering manna on the grass.
It dries, I know, and turns to sand
And ebbs away within the glass;

I know the green blood and the red
Drain back into the thirsty earth
Turning the great wheel of the dead
Upon the waters of rebirth:

They do not know, who share with me
From that hard course this hour's release,
In time we all must make return ...
Now Spirit, smile, and give us peace.

Japanese prints

You are lovelier
than swans on winter water
frosted, mirrored, still.

You are lovelier
than a bough of white petals
blue spring wind fingered.

You are lovelier
than shadows richer than green
treed summer coinage.

You are lovelier
than autumn embers, sweeter
even than remembered silences.

The blackbird

I have remembered suddenly
A young morning when we met
And hand in hand upon the window sat
In the dew air before the sun was up
To hear a cool-throat blackbird sing.

Dawn no more than a grey scarf
Hung about the neck of night.
Light grew quietly, pearl
Between the breasts of morning.
The garden a green gown silver
Seeded with mist
Lay for the day to rise and wear
The lawn's level velvet.
The world was cool as running water.

Dew like candles beaded all branches.
Save in our hearts where the bubble of joy
Burst in showers of silver
Only the light moved
And only the blackbird
Set it to music.

Longer than wifelong

Do you who are wifelong loved
Feel my eyes upon you? If you do
Have you the pain which is love's recognition
From being watched, as I in watching you?

You do your task, head bowed, hair brown
Down slender neck and slim back bent
Teaching again what I from you have learnt
Of human grace
And, when I see your face
Of beauty, growing
Quiet as tears that flow by candlelight.

I as I watch you wish to keep you so
But longer than life and wifelong
If only by this act transcending time
I might translate you out of day and night
Growing older, smaller, burial
And give you like a star although long dead
An after age of loving light.

The workshed

Please come - do tread upon my road.
Let pass,
Lay on its side the deadly glass
Here mark time running in my blood.
Your understanding may explain
And so release this joylike pain
We to time's s top may do each other good.

This workshed is the place. Come in.
For this time's being rout
All thoughts of what you'd be about;
I'll lend my spirit's eyes till yours begin
To be awake. I only want to show
The poetry of things which by hands grow
Out of the dead wood new life win.

Oh, no - it is not nothing I have done
As yet not much, but trust:
I only stay you since there must
Between us pass the sense of things begun
Of shapes and uses in the fingers bred
New living lovely - as though saws and chisels
      bled
Into the wood, making creation one.

What quest or rest?

You are adrift. – I tell you
You are adrift and do not know it.

– Towards what bourne then are you going
In this no longer rimmed confusion?
Do you have lodestone, compass, map
Recognise stars to steer by?
What do you do when winds
Pull every which way whirling thoughts –
Let down your anchors? What anchors
Have you, engines, oars in case of breakdown
Lifeboats do you carry? Indeed
What flag or flags do you sail under –
Only old bones' anarchy and ending?

Let us change metaphors.
Unwrap your layers like Peer Gynt's onion.
– What heart have you that is really you?
At any given moment, stop! – say this I am
And hear your thoughts clash swords
While all your civil wars break out like eczema;
Then raddle up your brow
To perceive battles' end the morrow
Bevond tomorrow
When your spirit and your circumstances
Sign the grand peace.

Come then to the green table.
Leave seas and wars, turn lawyer, diplomat
Bargain the terms on which you will
Be what you become
(Rubbing your wants like shoulders on the bars
Of what you cannot do –
Upon what terms do caged beasts sign truce?).

Yet if they could I could you could
What choice between the warring selves
Would satisfy one's soul
Quell ferment, light up firmament
And in what quest or rest bring peace?

Two notes from hospital

1. Screams

In hospital hearing screams
Is part of the programme of reduction
Like road drills seeking worn foundations out:
The surface alarmingly thinner
Than faith or fear have found it.

So pain' s corruption
Under the shallow basement of the skin
Shrieks what narrow basis in the skull
The spirit that we build or bruise on keeps.

The surface of life is thinner
Than faith or fear have found it.

2. Across the ward

I want to sleep a short while only,
Being tired the way weariness seems
Not worth resisting,
But sitting on the bedside stop,
Ears bubbling with Harry's breathing

Who, crouched at his bed all morning fought,
Grew tired the way weariness was
Impossible resisting;
Hunched himself in, lay back, slowly
Lost trouble. Feet come falling in his breathing.

I feel I should not ape approaching death,
Life suddenly shrinking is
Too sad for wasting.
I try to tilt at time with words -
The feet arrive, and stop the breath.

All this day

I have had, all the day in my mind
The image of a cherry bough
With blossom as thick as hoar rind
As light as your breath now
As white as snow
– And why I do not know

Except that all day my mind's hand caught
At yours; and wondering what to say
This was the most delicate thought
I could find, and all this day
It persisted too:
It must have been meant for you.

Quantock Hills – an escape

Paper.
More paper.
Clamouring of things people
questions decisions
needed answers required
out of the brain's thickening
greyness.
Noise. Mess. Telephone's insolence.
Hurry worry irritable from
time's incessant drum.

Load the car with camp kit.
Fill the tank.
Head west
roadsides green and white.

Over the hills raingrey gathers.
Spots on the windscreen.
Stop by the five-bar gate
for the view's sweep and the wind's
brush in the hair.
The cows are lying down.

Road gathers under
rain overhead

                                        [wipers' ...

wipers' steady swishwash
the radio quartet's play
engine's thrum wind's rush
insulate the mind
only eyes and instincts on the winding way.

Halt – up some quiet offroad
narrow hillsided always
coppice and hedgerow to see.
Quietness collects the other thoughts for
storage. Lay them by. Have
food and drink; music if wished ...

The spattering rain again.
Drive on, the colours fading
rain steadier
tyres hissing.
Lights go on
windscreen a jeweller's in passing headlamps;
watch the white lines
the climbing beam beyond the hill
signposts
the gauge.

Listen to the news
war assassination strikes
demonstrations violence
rebellion born of rebelliousness.

Grateful for music following:
against the rain slash engine hum
the great chords state their truth.

Watch the signposts, watch –

turn left here.   And here.
And here again.
Narrow, climbing
a gulley between high
hedges and Queen Anne's lace
headlights slapping the bends
the road swaying right left
rain slanting in the beams
blackness beyond
no houses now.

Climb still and swing the wheel
and dip and turn
to find the one right road
tiredness hitting the head.

The last turn
up the rocky path
the tunnel of boughs –
and here the glade, forest behind,

[the open...

the open down
the valley below's dark bed.

Sit still.
Sit quietly
engine and lights off.
Listen.
Be still,
only the night moving
with wind and rain
and splattering boughs.

Then light dim in the car
and food and water to wash;
a cramped undressing
a sleeping bag in the back
stretch out
cigarette wireless drink
sleep
in the pouring dark ...

Soft swords into the sleeping eyes
the early sun.
At the ears the birds enter.

Listen, be glad, but
turn and sleep again

until the swords and songs both say
'now peace is in awakening.'

Last night's rain washed yesterday away.
Lie and look and listen to now.
Stretch and rise and dress.
Wash cold shave brisk
dowse head slosh shoulders
brush teeth make water
sing.

Sun in glory, clouds in flotilla
sail the mothering deep.
Shadow flecks the glade
the wet grass warms.

Prepare the stove, the kettle:
eggs and bacon sizzle
water boils
the air grows hungry.
Eat.
Sit in the climbing sun
drinking the last sweet tea
with a slow cigarette to conjure
the comfortable presence of smoke.

[Clear...

Clear away.
Light the pipe.
Shirt off sit back shut eyes
the sun fire on flesh
orange behind the eyelids.

Cuckoo and blackbird thrush
and lofted lark
make only their own comment.
We relate without bondage.

The shadows move across the valley.
On a distant farm a dog barks.

I grow in the greengold sun
the wind in the woods and on my shoulders
and begin to write my thanks.

Remembering former friends

Birds call
rain tingles on the window,
Under the grey all green growths flourish,
The piano is wistful on the wireless.

Strange how some
sudden essence of combining senses
recollects friends
from the mind's past shore on which they lie
like boats no longer kept in good repair
by seas no longer sailed upon
in harbours which have ceased
to feel my feet approach the quay.

Stranger to know
they're not the empty shells my mind reflects.
No doubt their gear is trim
their hulls as sound as age allows.
They tack those reaches still perhaps
or sail on other seas like me
new courses set
with new companions helping at their sails.

[What...

What other landfalls have they made
I wonder, since I sailed with them?
What new horizons turned towards?

And shall we by our separate ways
arrive beyond the world's last rim
and ever know again what we have been
share what we became.

The marriage tie

The vow it is I think, that
Sticks in the moral craw
Emotional gullet;
Stops the swallow of some
Numbing forgetfulness, or
The finally shut door.

What else than love –
And which came first or lasts? –
So obstinate should glue
Disparate surfaces of mind and soul
Together, try to make
Selfwayward paths congrue
Towards some mutual yet
Uncommon goal?

Huge vistas of relationships unroll
To my mind's half blind eye:
'Where do they come from
Where do they go?' their ghost train
In my night shrieks – 'Why?'
And rumbles, fading, only
An imagined smoke trail
Registering, and veiling
Huge questions unanswered
Insoluble chemistry.

Enoch Powell

I heard a radio interview today.
The girl's light voice, prefabricated ploys.
Strategic inferences, scarce concealed
What, prematurely, eagerness revealed:
The central plan to rouse a public noise
From personal confrontation, so betray
Her seeming sympathies of confidence.
The trap was crude. The politician knew it.
Instead the scholar, soldier, teacher, poet
Spoke, as before the harsher presidence
Of judgement by that inner court above
Where fellowship, reason, laughter, joy, grief,
       love
As jurors sit – to insist the final word
Be true, and understood not simply heard.

Jacob returns

Traveling home
I am no shadow speaking mouth

Brain wrestled with the angel by the way
To make words truth
My bell tower ladder rung by rung
Aspires

But now I walk with a disjointed gait
Mastered for ways no more my own
Speaking what I have seen

To earn my name
By what is
That is known

Summer's gone

The summer's gone since last we met
He said. Less than a week ago.
That's true. It happens so
Upon a sudden unexpected day.

It had been long and hot and driving dry.
The flowers had drooped before they bloomed
Corn grew only half-way up the cob
The grass was parched.
Flower-beds dried, grew hard and cracked
With fissures one could put a hand into.
Real rain – we'd had a palmful over months.
The bonus was to walk in shorts
And barefoot sandals, browning in the sun –
Paid for with sweat though, hours of watering,
Forks which bit the thrusting not the ground.

Then, of a September day, first soft rain found
Its so-long misdirected way to us;
A wind sprang up
And from the colding north blew down dried
    leaves;
The apples bombed upon the yellow grass
Unready yet for plucking.
The sun had lost its warmth; the legs
Grew trousers as the air grew chill.

And looking out the window, I felt
Winter at the sill
So sudden
Fragile – with the brown upon me and
The summer in me still.

Clocks go back

The clocks are back
Two days gone – still
I can't get round to it: the mill
Of time revolves on summer hours
When grinding autumn gold.
I shall get used to winter's white and black
Its boney cold
The morning window's frozen flowers;

But I was digging round the silver birch
The day clocks closed the summer down –
I'd quite forgotten having sown
Beneath the tangle I was forking out
Narcissi, snowdrops, crocuses.
It's odd – I've registered before
How digging focuses
The spirit's obstinately endless search
For hopeful signs of what life's all about.

No doubt it needn't be admired
(Signs do most often go together)
And yet it touched me deeper than the eye
That when I took the dog a walk, smirrh
        weather
Today at dusk, testing the novel clock,

Both damp-drip earth and greyspit sky
Glowed russet yet with setting summer fired.

I need – don't you? – both backlook sigh
And the buried bulb-growth's shock.

Things unsaid

Things unsaid
Are sometimes lovelier
– That the tongue was shy of
And even the eyes shunned.
Something between us nevertheless
Moved like water
Rang like bells.

There was no great metallic crash;
No peals explored the great rings' range:
But you no more than me would have been
    fooled
Knowing what notes, though never called,
Each sensed within the other's singing steeple.

By things unsaid we are no longer strange,
Never again quite separate people.

Triptych

What one should see is clearer...

Who should walk countries
Especially by boughs bud breaking
Without now more than ever
Stretching out hands to touch creation
That soon might never
Again spring green and gold and
Sticky like blood.

Remember so clearly the boy I
Was with a switch and a swishing off
Cow parsley, dandelion heads –
Loved to destroy.
I cannot, could never repeat
That abandon of thanks.

And not growing older or wiser
I know when I see how the rest of me warps
Has made me aware.
I'm just fuller of fear
And fuller of hopes.

[be...

be is nearer...

One comes by keeping open only
To what one can say:
No other how so straight a way
To what we should also do.

Too labyrinthine wise we are
To care or see
What is as plain as day:
What when we face it cries joy
Weeps dismay
Or orders Stoic grit.

To see the right way
Needs an unmasked light.
But standing before it
We cast our own shadow
Make our own night.

say is shorter.

Time.
We who must go pray God
Give us quiet leave
Not what we might deserve
Of furious fire or fearful lime
Nor foolish fuss.
Dignity the greatest have
Earned for each of us.

When the eye listens

When the eye listens
The tongue is blinded.
How should it speak green
Of turquoise leaves and falling waters seen
Or tell the pendulous purple of a fuchsia bell's
Stifled carillon?
I grow dumber, older,
Pondering how.

But why – I know, have heard
The brief but silver trumpets of man's fight
Enlist for trial by pen and word
Meaning's day and matter's night –
Ordeal of battle every inward mind
Fights with frail weapons of its outward sight.

Yet I perceive all speech
Like all translation
Is defeat
– Or just so slight a foothold for that mind
Wary on foreign matter.
By shallow tricks of talk the tongue is only
Part master of the depthless, speechless thing.

What astonishes is that
Momentary is what we need not be
Since we can last as long
As men can read and sing:
It gives unending value to unfinished strife –

All life
Like all language
Is so magnificent a disaster.

The Somme, 1918

Just a few years before my birth
Blood a battery against the sounds of death
Before they thought again for what, upon a
    breath
They turned to shattered laurel on the earth.

We now at third thoughts only with folly's
    shame
Should wear upon our minds their thorns of
    pain
Who, if their silence moved again
Would mock us, and with stripped bones blame.

Come peaceful

Discharge the armies of my disarray
Which turn from civil forays on my hopes
To plunder purposes heart kept, and bray
Across my sleep their trumpets of dismay.

If you – bring blessed things to please
This tyrant anguish and my martial fears: a
    smile
A touch, or words to knit the mind's torn ease
With meaning's reconciling guile.

If not – despatch that spirit by which I
Can set the eyes to search again
For lights within my stormy sky
And ears to hear some song behind its rain.

Thought water

I need a pool of thought
to dip my mind in
cool and clear and sweetly springing
from some deep source on some high mountain.

There is no pool unless I make one
from depths of spirit in the heights of mind.
It will only be cool if I am clear
only as clear as my own seeing
only as deep as my own loving
only as high as my own thinking.

It seems a last reality
necessary to truth
to recognise what living water
can only be drawn from one's own well
and nothing comes out
of nothing put in.

Of course it is not I alone
who conjure rain into my earth
or trickle truth and understanding in;
but I am sand to parch my givers
thin earth which gives scant blessing back –

yet I have caves
and through my fissured rock
slowly the water gathers in my dark ...

I wish
it lay less deep and more accessible
I wish it lay upon the mountain side
and had the colour of the sky –
in which to bathe would be to fly.

Things undone

Things undone
though wanted to be
press on the – not so much mind
as spirit –
oppress with the passing of
time unsatisfied
foreknowledge of ending it so.

Small most things perhaps, uncaught,
adrift for want of effort, care or thought
or much worse will,
though on time's ebb haunt us still
more than what we more certainly forsook –

a view uncaptured, camera not brought
let alone sketch-book;
new insight
that vanished for a penless note:
the half remembered uncompleted quote,
the recommended title yet unread,
music's unfollowed nor regained delight:
a morning's sunshine dulled to showers
before that pleasing usefulness which might
have walked the dog, made good the shed
or cleaned the windows which the sun ashamed.

Letters unwritten,
friendships unrepaired.
Plays, concerts, matches, exhibitions
missed.
Paintings unpainted
poems uncomposed
the song unsung, the empty stave.
The plant unrescued weakly dying
for the remembered then forgotten drink
seed trays barren of next summer's flowers
the unkissed lover husband wife
and all
uncelebrated unremembranced days:
a myriad stifled messages to life
we carry in us struggling to the grave
unbaptised and unshriven
incomplete, un-named.

Too much! Too much you'll cry
to do – we are not sainted!
True.
More for not better trying
than not doing I think
we shall be blamed.

Absolution

one sin – to call a green leaf grey – Chesterton.

"It might be Autumn" I suggest.
Sky dull, air damp, ground wet,
A long wind lofty in the trees   (And yet
I know that Spring feels like a ringdove's
    breast.)

You say – "there's something warm within the
    grey,
A light behind it too – you see?"
I do not, though I sense it true. We
Walk. But I am winter tired. The day

"Might just as well be Autumn" I repeat
With obstinate fatigue. "To call a green leaf
    grey?"
You softly quote. "It's *not* an Autumn day;
Don't be so wilful blind. Let's greet

Together all the signs we can of Spring –
Look at that bud unfurling on the bush,
And on those trees the faintly, greening flush ..."
You pause; I hear a blackbird sing.

In March lark country

In March lark country
Lifting smooth contours,
Swelling out of barren time,
Where soared some singing
Daft with the first burnish –
Over the hill's brow, down valley
Far away shots fired.

What in this blue and umber
Green becoming empire
Came to nothing?
Stunned sudden
Ears split blood spilling
While all above the misty birds
Still laughed like crikey
Over the green grass soaking up
Sun gold.

Easter sun

When cloud shrouds shredded by the wind
Disclose the risen body of the sun
And cartographic cherubs are imagined
Blowing lively barques on
A thriving trade run

The image of the quiet white angel is discarded
– that guarded solemnly the breathless tomb –
This side of heaven seems enough awarded
And demanded for whoever's from
Only a man pierced womb.

Birthday walk

I collected wood on my birthday
Late afternoon of lovely weather
Walking the bluebell drifted hanger,
From moss and mast
Retrieving broken beech bits.

Tinder dry, that night
I burnt my birthday walk
And it again grew bright.

Surely, my wife said,
You've been good
To end and start a year of life
With such a sight
Of green and gold and blue and white.
Not so, I fear and know.
But to have been born in May
Is luck enough to start a path;
However muddy it becomes
Each yearly birth resows it green –

I take it, through the newling woods
The sunlight showers of the leaves
The spattered shadows on the lazy
Waves of dream-hued, drifting, hazy
                              [Earth-borne...

Earth-borne clouds
Whose silent un-rung blue compels
The answering quietness and the eyes' slow
gaze.

Who would have thought that clamouring
Spring
Busy for nature's noisy people
With wind and bird hymn building a green
church
Could hush and hang for our amaze
So still a peal within its thrusting steeple?

We wandered slowly, dog and I – both
Snuffing the different smells we sought:
Beech-mould for me would surely do
But subtler sniffs from other feet,
No presence left that I could sense,
Invited her. I walked alone and unaware
Of other than her errant company
And that of my new year and passing years.
The downing sun felt gold and good
On my back, bent for bits of bough
As I climbed out of the bell-bound wood.
Later, we sat by candlelight
With music round us in the air
And evening curtains half drawn on the night.
Feeding the last fire with my old year's fuel,

The sense of summer coming,
I saw my birthday walking in the blaze
Its greengold redgold turning ...

I do not know
And feel I should not care
If it was Spring or Autumn
I watched
Burning.

Ideas

Sometimes they come unexpected –
Ideas as clean as blessings:
Phrases, sentences, clues; keys
To doors to corridors with doors
And suddenly by passages of sight
To halls of understanding
Sunshot domes of light.

I never know why. Wherefrom
Puzzles me infinitely.
They come like birds with beaks of
Olive branches to my ark
From lands of hope and guesswork.

(If shot - an albatross of words
It may be or may seem no more
However others find it gives rewards;
If not – a flake from flying snows
That crystal came but shapeless goes.
How rare the bird which nestles, branch that
    grows.)

I don't expect to reach their shore
But I can send their signal from my ark
Into the dark.

Nothing lovelier

Nothing is lovelier than the sudden smile
Translating the formal morning's greetings,
Evening partings, casual passings
With a will to warmth.

More than the hand's help, soft or firm,
That smile gives strength
Digestible and quickening
Natural as honey.

I would rather you smiled in passing
Making the face flower that I might be refreshed
Than be welcomed with service
Or warmed with praise
However yearned or earned and won –

The smile is something meant for me
That only you have done.

The lecture room

Suddenly, waking, I was
caught so strongly with the thought
of you, that I could turn back time to when
across the lecture room – how long?
so many years ago? and yet
so sharply seen and sensed to me
both now as then, I'd walk into that place
that long long time – for so it seems –
and frame of mind any today
at the flick of a will...

Across the upturned faces, black
gowns, occasional pencils, scarves,
between the desk rows under the barrel roof
before the old man on the dais
trousers at half-mast, shuffling, witty,
talking illiterate medieval kings,
and clearly, sharply through the murmurs,
      laughs
cutting the atmospherics of the crowd
I looked and looked and loved you
all alone
we might have been
though bound in separate places...
and centuries of history lay
unlistened to between our faces.

Panic and pain

Of course lifelong I had been finding
thoughts, or they found me.
But suddenly
it seemed I crossed a frontier to a land
as rich as spring with newnesses and
no more frontiers.
There
ideas like races to be run tore
open panic lest they should be lost
and beat like tides about the swiftening blood.

This is no land of milk and honey quiet.
Only the restless searchers come
here drawing words like water from
deep wells below their spirits' hills:
to whom the printed page becomes
a joy too much like pain
yearning to be given
in others
birth again.

Pilgrim's rest
Gappas Llwyd – Field of the Grey Cloaks

Here over centuries, between six still peaks
of grass and granite and the ever restless
sounding surf, pilgrims rested
peacefully prayed and
travelled on in hope
for the last lap.

Garments weighted with rain and mud
dried partly overnight whilst they
slept heavy as tired eyelids.
Before light someone stirred their dreams
– kindly, by the feel of the place;
they woke stiffly, washed with chill water,
broke fast meagrely, and strode
leaving thanks and any alms they might
(which rest upon the land)
up to the saddle between rival peaks
(their narrow path still wears worn stones).

Below beyond the ridge the flattening land
spread dark into the sea
grey as their garments.
Left, on the rim of the world's platter
light broke like bread:
they paused, the wind cold on their faces,

quietly communicant as dawn spilt
wine over heaving sea and heavy rock.

Eyes strained, they could see the Holy Isle
far off, but smiled with more than hope
and looking at each other
walked lighter down the further slope.

In the language of eyes

In the language of eyes only
Have I truly spoken to you.

What is unsaid between us grew
No other image than our own.
The private view
Is not confused with expectation;
We do not have to reap
What words have never sown.

It has puzzled me to know
When fetus becomes person.
The stillborn baby is a life unopened,
But like a thought unspoken
Neither was always dead –
And more
They share a kind of immortality,
Children unborn and words unsaid.

Accounts due

God says everything has to be paid for
– You must get it into your head
Everything has to be paid for:
You'll pay for your life when you're dead.

But, lest you let 'live now pay later'
Complacently cause you to thrive,
First settle with Man and with Nature –
You'll still pay for your life whilst alive!

My wife often says daft things

My wife often says
quite daft things.
"How lovely to do that" she
suddenly said. –
The candles had guttered
(we dine by their light)
and before they were quite dead
I had replaced them
natural as night.

In amaze
but beguiled
"What on earth
do you mean?"
I asked her.   She smiled
with soft mirth
and said – "Well they were dead
you've put new ones instead.
It's a kind of rebirth,
that's what I've seen,
turning nights into days."

My wife often says
quite daft things
because her mind sings.

Cease, decrease, increase

Why bother?
God?
Why worry?
Seek heaven? –
Here's a cheap one:
Nothing
Anyway, nothing to pay.
Listen:
Be very, very
STILL.

Between that full
STOP
And this again beginning
There must have been
Peace
There must have been
Wonder.

If not go back and
Wonder why.

It's as good a start as any.

And it doesn't cost a

John Torrance

Dimensions of remembrance
in memoriam D.H.

I know now *where* you are –
this flagstone set in grass
with motto, name and honours,
if it were made of glass,
would show your urn in the ground
and that, if a crystal vase,
would show, inside, exactly
how little now must pass
for you, in this our fourfold
scheme of things, this bare
vast scaffolding of worlds,
three quarters of it 'where' –
and how your best is nowhere now.

Do I know *when* you are?
Beyond these ashes, nowhere
is not to say no-when.
The stone tells times you were –
your 'when' must still embrace
those years of then and there –
but why not more, much more
than that brief fling with 'where'?
Who knows the rules? If not

pegged down by place to a date,
can 'when' be large as time,
Wandering early and late,
Could you be with us, even now?

I do know *what* you are.
for me – and what will stay:
the one who never said
I'd come too late to play,
but brought out all the toys
you'd almost put away,
and revelled in the zest
of rivalrous display.
Still my first encourager,
your words a tempered wind
to my shorn lambs, begetter
of my autumnal spring –
your voice all letters, poems, now.

2004

Martin Dace

In memoriam David Henschel

The day's last light refracted in the glass
Of home-made wine: elder, secret herbs,
And conversation. From his learnèd garden
Knowledge like flowers, the roundnesses of
     words,
And humour in his eyes: the civilised
Accompaniments to seeking the profound.

And here we are:
"Oh do enjoy! The hereness and the nowness of
     it!"

The thing we sought, we had, we always have,
Which has no name in Newton's, Einstein's
     world:
The place where the eternal now cuts
The closed world of our senses five
And lives forever.

Norah Henschel

Elderflower wine

Every Summer we do this,
Milking the rich curds from the hedgerow
To start a different journey through this year
To next year
Some time alchemical marrying.
Persephone and Dionysus wed
Here at the edge of the hayfield.

Druids cut the magic plant
With golden sickles.
Our hands, gold-dusted,
Solemnise this matrimony.

Child of this day's conceiving
Shall flow honey-gold in goblets,
Its fragrance bring to mind again
The pleasure of this gathering;
Poised between memory and expectation,
We penetrate a shadowless present,
Because every Summer we do this.

Norah Henschel

Husbandman David

He in his hilltop garden
Conjures the seasons.
Cloud and wind and rain and the blissful sun
Circle his head like an aureole
Heavy and gentle he treads the earth
Like Adam;
Sits by the stars and sings.

He in the shadowed room,
Smoke-fragrant, candle-soft, dreams
Of order, music, dust, and friends and voices;
Gathers, like Puck, the day's diversities,
And mends the fire for Lob.

And he is Merlin, husbanding mysteries;
Swings upon the airy planes of thought,
Trapezing:
Heals his wound with words
And flings them forth as bread
To break with friends
For comfort.

*Editor's note: Lob is the household spirit of the hearth
in folklore*

Afterthought
from David Henschel's *Quantock Hills*

Listen, be glad, but
turn and sleep again
until the swords and songs both say
'now peace is in awakening.'

❧

Lightning Source UK Ltd.
Milton Keynes UK
05 September 2010
159436UK00006B/13/P